THE CIVIL WAR HANDBOOK

How to Dress, Talk, Eat, and
Command like a
CONFEDERATE CAPTAIN

Robin Robinson

SILVERLEAF
PRESS

Silverleaf Press Books are available exclusively
through Independent Publishers Group.

For details write or telephone
Independent Publishers Group, 814 North Franklin St.
Chicago, IL 60610, (312) 337-0745

Silverleaf Press
8160 South Highland Drive
Sandy, Utah 84093

CONTENTS

THE WAR BEGINS

In the year 1860 the United States was still a nation, but it was a deeply divided one. Much had changed since the thirteen colonies had come together in a spirit of compromise to forge a new government and a new country of freedom less than one hundred years before. Colonies became states, settlers moved west, and citizens with a vision for the future flourished in new times of growth and opportunity. But gradually the two parts of this nation, the North and the South, developed very differently. The South was an area dominated by rich agriculture, with cotton being the primary crop. The North was industrial and had many factories. Steamboats transported goods throughout the nation and across the Atlantic to Europe.

The differences in these two economies, however, were not enough to cause a war by themselves. Another issue that raised strong feelings on both sides was that of slavery. The South needed many workers to pick and process their cotton; the cheapest and easiest way for them to do this was by using slave labor. But

Jefferson Davis, the president of the Confederacy

slavery was unfair and often cruel to blacks. Many in the North raised their voices for abolition—a call to abolish the practice of slavery by making it illegal.

As is often the case in history, certain events transpired that shifted what was already a delicate balance

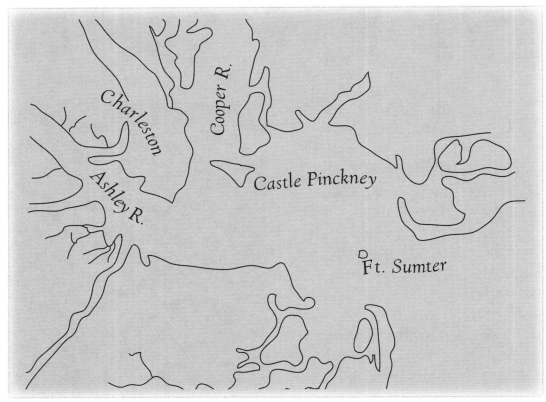

Map of Fort Sumter.

decisively in one direction. In this case there were, among others, two very important events. First, in 1859 an abolitionist named John Brown from the North attempted to start a revolt among the slaves by leading a group of them in an attack on a federal arsenal. Slave owners started to feel nervous about whether other groups of slaves would revolt. If that happened, the slave owners would be outnumbered and overpowered, losing their lands and incomes—indeed, their whole way of life. Second, Abraham Lincoln, a man whom many Southerners viewed as against slavery, was elected as the sixteenth president of the United States. As soon as they heard about Lincoln's election, representatives from seven Southern states joined together to secede from the United States, forming the Confederate States of America. The combined army from these states declared war on the North by firing on Fort Sumter, a national fort in South Carolina built to protect the Charleston harbor. When four other Southern states heard about this united act of violence, they decided to secede and join the Confederacy. The war had begun.

COMMISSIONS

1

Having been born and raised in the state of Virginia, you are a true Southerner and your state is dear to your heart. Your graduation day at the Virginia Military Institute last year, June of 1860, was a proud one for your entire family, and everyone from your grandparents to the newest baby was there to see you receive your honors. In recent months, family dinner discussions have become quite heated as everyone in your family feels strongly about the need for an independent Southern government. The Northern states seem utterly unsympathetic to the needs of the South, and many view secession as the only answer. Soon you hear of the formation of the Confederate States of America and an attack on Fort Sumter in South Carolina.

A letter arrives in the mail one day, and from it you learn that one of your favorite instructors from the Academy is now serving as a colonel for the Confederate Army. What's more, he has remembered you as one of the outstanding students of your class at VMI, and has asked you to accept a commission as a captain under his command. You are highly honored and determined to do your best to serve both the Southern states and this man whom you respect so much.

COMMISSIONED OFFICERS

During the Civil War, commissioned officers were the chief leaders of the Southern army. As chief decision-makers, they held specific positions of authority and were the only individuals in the military officially authorized to issue commands.

Commissioned officers typically had attended a military training school. There were several of these in the United States at the time, including the United States Military Academy at West Point, the United States Naval Academy, the Virginia Military Institute, and the Citadel. Jefferson Davis, President of the United States of the Confederacy, created a new Confederate Naval Academy for the appointment and training of cadet infantry officers. West Point led all the other schools in the number of graduates it contributed to the armies of both the North and the South. Commissioned officers held a rank of 2nd lieutenant or above in the army.

NONCOMMISSIONED OFFICERS

Noncommissioned officers were appointed to their commission without undergoing generalized military training, although some had undergone specialized training. They were officially authorized to have control or charge of their troops, rather than having "command" of them. During the Civil War, men were appointed to commissions for various reasons: they might have recruited other soldiers, or sometimes their advancement was necessary due to loss of leaders' lives in battle. If they were specialists in a specific area of the military, they could have authority because of their expertise.

Enlisted personnel who had either volunteered or were conscripted (drafted), made up the bulk of soldiers in the army. They were not appointed to a commission unless they advanced through the army ranks.

West Point cadets marching to dinner.

UNIFORMS

The uniforms used by the Confederate army varied a great deal. Some of the differences distinguished one rank from another. But often, even soldiers in the same unit would have uniforms with different styles and details simply because there was no centralized plan or place to produce the uniforms.

Whatever their differences, the majority of the Confederate army clothes themselves in grey (as opposed to the Union army's blue). The soldier's insignia was placed on his collar to help others know his rank in the army. Confederate officers wore gold braiding, or "frogging," sewn on their sleeves in a pattern called the "Austrian knot."

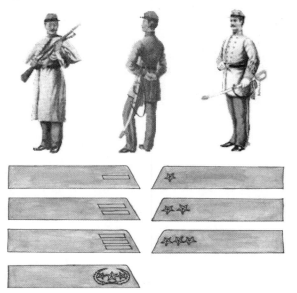

Top: Uniforms of a Confederate private, captain, and major. Bottom: Collar insignia (left to right): Second Lieutenant, Major, First Lieutenant, Lieutenant Colonel, Captain, Colonel, General

Issuing Commands Like a Commissioned Officer

You will need:
Paper
A quill pen
Ink

Imagine that you are a general or other commissioned officer. Think about what you would like your troops to do—move to a new camp? Divide in half and execute a surprise attack on the enemy? Addressing you comments to your supporting officers, write copies of your orders and send them with spies or agents.

How to Make a Quill Pen and Ink

You will need:
A large feather (about 6 inches or longer)
A small, sharp knife

Holding the feather carefully, shave off the bottom inch of feathering so that the quill is smooth. This is where you will hold the feather pen to write. (Always have adult permission and supervision when you use a knife.) Follow the illustrations in order to create the tip of your pen. Instructions for making berry ink and invisible ink are on the following page.

Berry Ink

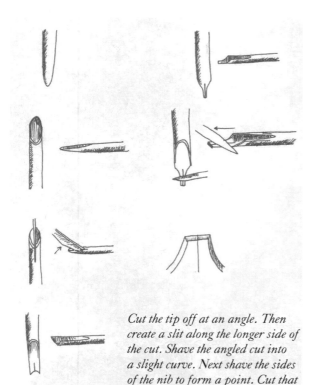

You will need:
- ½ Cup fresh berries
- ½ teaspoon vinegar
- ½ teaspoon salt

1. Crush berries and push them through a strainer so the juice is pulp free.
2. Mix with vinegar and salt. You can use a glass baby food jar as an "inkwell."

Invisible Ink

You will need:
- Lemon juice
- A toaster

1. Use a Q-tip to write with lemon juice.
2. Send it to a friend, with instructions to hold the paper over the toaster to heat it up. Make sure the paper does not get too hot, just warm. The writing should appear as it heats.

Cut the tip off at an angle. Then create a slit along the longer side of the cut. Shave the angled cut into a slight curve. Next shave the sides of the nib to form a point. Cut that point off at an angle to create the tip of the pen.

How to Make a Confederate Jacket

Now that you have your commission, the first thing you do to get ready to leave is ask the local tailor to make you a uniform. Unfortunately he's swamped with work, but he offers to help you make your own.

Supplies:
- *1 small grey suit coat*
- *14– 16 brass buttons*
- *Buttons or appliqué material for the collar (see collar illustration on p. 5 for shapes)*
- *Strip of yellow or gold material, long enough to reach around your waist*
- *Gold tassels for ends of sash, if desired*
- *Gold cord for the Austrian knot*

1. Fold the collar up of the suit coat and fold over the lapels. Sew the buttons up the front in two rows, three to four inches apart.
2. Sew the buttons or appliqués on the collar.
3. Follow the instructions for the Austrian knot (see below) and sew them to your jacket sleeves.
4. If you would like, sew the tassels to the end of your sash. Put the jacket on and tie the sash around your waist.

Instructions for the Austrian knot:

Pin the gold braid onto the jacket sleeve, following the steps as illustrated. Stitch carefully, preferably by hand, along the edges of the gold braid. Make sure the entire length of the braid is securely fastened down so it won't snag or come undone.

The Austrian knot.

8

LIFE IN CAMP

2

Your Civil War camp is like a large, busy city of white tents. It is filled with soldiers, some busily tending to their duties and others lounging about. The air is thick with the smoke from hundreds of campfires. Your camp is considered temporary throughout the year until the winter months when you will set up more permanent winter quarters. Camp life differs widely from soldier to soldier and from camp to camp, but there are many elements of camp life that are the same for everyone.

Since most battle engagements occur during the summer months (actually late spring through early fall), you use your time differently in summer camps. During the winters, battles are the exception rather than the rule. Summers find you traveling light, ready to move, and never knowing what tomorrow will bring. Winters mean long hours with none of the terror or excitement of battle, and every day is spent in much the same way. If you are granted furlough (pronounced fir-low), you can leave camp for a time to visit home and family, but for most soldiers, furlough was only a wish and never a reality.

SUPPLIES AND SUTLERS

If a soldier ran out of any supplies, he couldn't simply drop in to the nearest town to visit the grocery or hardware store—even if he happened to have any money (which was unlikely). The soldier could write home and ask his family to send the needed items, but then he would have to wait several weeks for the letter to even reach home. By the time a package arrived, the camp may have relocated, or even headed off to battle. Consequently, most of the time troops were forced to rely on the camp sutler, an army-sanctioned salesman who set up temporary shop near camps and battlegrounds to offer toiletries,

A sutler's cart selling papers.

canned fruit, pocketknives, and other goods for sale—but usually at terribly high prices.

SHELTER

Although there were several types of tents used during the Civil War, most soldiers were issued the pup or "dog" tent, so nicknamed because the soldiers joked that only a dog could crawl under it and stay dry from the rain.

Each soldier was issued one shelter half, which he carried when on the march and then joined with the half of another soldier when it was time to set up camp for the night. The two halves buttoned together along the top ridge. To pitch the tent, two posts were set up (if the soldiers could not find wood from fences or trees they would often just use their guns, with bayonets attached, sticking them down into the ground) with a short rope strung between the posts and the tent draped ever

Here, on a large plain, surrounded by an amphitheater of bluffs, were collected about 70,000 of our troops, presenting from the high ground a most magnificent sight. On all sides but the north there were tents,—high marquees for the officers, and low shelter-tents for the men. To the northward was the river with its gunboats....In every other direction...there was a solid mass of tents and artillery and wagons, extending to a great distance. Twenty square miles were...covered by that camp.[1]

the rope. There was no tent floor, no front or back flap. The longer the soldiers used their leaky, drafty tents ,the more they came up with new and unusual ways to set them up.

Officers were more commonly issued marquee (pronounced mar-key) tents, which were larger and taller than the pup tents. These bigger tents allowed officers to be more

Various styles of tents would be found within a camp.

An example of a tent set up using poles.

comfortable in their quarters. They had room for a writing desk, a cot, and perhaps a trunk or two for military paperwork and supplies in addition to personal belongings. The larger size also afforded the officers a sheltered place to confer in private over confidential matters such as battle plans or troop discipline.

A stockaded tent.

When tents were unavailable, worn out, or had been discarded by

the infantry (usually during the summer months, when carrying them around was heavy and inconvenient), the troops had to cobble together makeshift dwellings to protect themselves from the elements. In summer they constructed lean-tos out of canvas or oilcloth, supported and sheltered by some branches or fence-rail frameworks. They called these creations "shebangs."

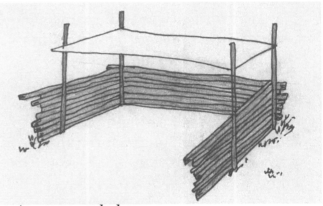
A summer shebang.

This Confederate camp has built more permanent structures to prepare for the oncoming winter.

In winter, when the troops would be staying in their camp for several months to wait out the bad weather, they built a "stockaded" tent by digging a hole down into the earth and then laying a rough wood or stone floor. Logs chinked with mud would then be set around the perimeter, over which the soldiers would build a wooden frame, stretching the tent across the top in teepee fashion.

TENT FURNISHINGS

The soldiers who wintered in their tents came up with creative ways to make the place a little more like home. They made wooden crates into tables or shelves and used sawed off stumps for chairs. Nails held canteens and haversacks. Bayonets were candlesticks. Many men created mattresses to avoid sleeping on the ground, and would stuff a pillow with straw or pine needles.

How to Make Your Own Straw or Pine Needle Stuffed Pillow

You will need:
An armful or two of dry pine needles or dry grass
1 yard muslin fabric
Scissors
Thread
Sewing machine (could also be sewn by hand)
An Iron

Collect pine needles or long dry grass from an empty field. Let air-dry for several days, turning them over and checking for insects or other foreign matter. Meanwhile, purchase a yard of muslin from a fabric store. Cut the fabric to measure 36 inches by 18 inches. Fold fabric in half, wrong side out, and sew the three raw edges in a continuous seam, leaving a 4-inch opening in one side. Clip corners so it will have less fabric when you turn it right side out. Reverse fabric, turning right side out. Press seams flat once again, making sure to fold in and iron edges of opening. Stuff the pillow with needles or grass, keeping the material to the center of the pillow, away from the edges. Finish by stitching all the way around the four edges of the pillow, 1/4 inch in from the edge.

FATIGUE DUTY

Your least favorite part of camp life is fatigue duty. You thought that by leaving home and heading off to war you would escape the chores that plagued you at home. But there are tasks that must be done in order to keep the camp functioning, and it seems to you that the work has no end.

At roll call the soldiers were assigned fatigue duties to perform. Chief among them was obtaining wood and water. All the campfires needed enormous supplies of wood to keep them burning, and everyone needed water whether for cooking, washing, or drinking. Other camp duties included cleaning and preparing guns and ammunition; keeping metal, wood, and leather equipment polished and functioning; clearing fields for parade or drills; and—perhaps most unpopular— guard duty. Guard duty required long hours of standing watch, day and night, rain or shine, on the alert for hostile troops or spies. It was cold, lonely, and boring, but if in boredom a soldier happened to doze off, the punishment could be severe.

LETTERS, PACKAGES, AND PHOTOGRAPHS

For those soldiers who could read and write, letters were the only means of communication. They were carefully saved to be read and reread many times. Writing letters was a way for soldiers to pass the long hours in camp, and they were the only way for folks back home to know about a soldier's new experiences—or for the soldier to know about theirs. The day mail arrived at camp was a day for celebration.

This sketch of the inside of an officer's tent contains some interesting details. Notice how the furnishings look more like a permanent home with a writing desk, wall hangings, and even a small table bar.

Those who received letters went off with radiant countenances.... If it was night, each built a fire for light and, sitting down on the ground, read his letter over and over. Those unfortunates who got none went off looking as if they had not a friend on earth.[2]

Letters the soldiers received would often tell of the hardships their families were facing back at

> *We're tenting on the old camp ground,*
> *Give us a song to cheer*
> *Our weary hearts, a song of home,*
> *And friends we love so dear.*
> *Many are the hearts that are*
> *Weary tonight,*
> *Wishing for the war to cease;*
> *Many are the hearts that are*
> *Looking for the right,*
> *To see the dawn of peace.*
> *Tenting tonight, tenting tonight,*
> *Tenting on the old camp ground.*
>
> *From the song "Tenting Tonight on the Old Camp Grounds," by Walter Kitteredge, c. 1862.*

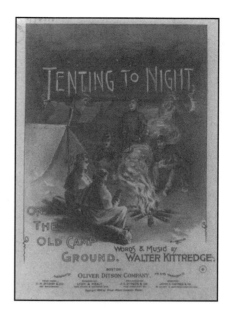

home. A difficult challenge for many families was obtaining enough food to eat. Faced with war shortages, they wrote to their sons, brothers, and husbands telling of creative substitutions for foods that the war had made scarce or unavailable.

Paper was usually in short supply during the war, so letter-writers wrote on any kind of paper they could find, even wallpaper, and sometimes even wrote crossways and in between their other writing.

In contrast to mail sent during other periods of conflict, letters mailed during the Civil War were uncensored and often contained both sensitive military information and deeply personal messages. (An exception to this was mail from prisoners of war, which usually was censored.)

Packages were a special delight, and often contained items the soldier had requested in his last letter home.

Liquor was usually forbidden in the army, but soldiers' families came up with highly creative ways of supplying their loved ones with a bit of "stimulating beverage."

Matthew B. Brady was the most famous photographer in America. He hired many other photographers who traveled throughout the North

> *Items Requested in Letters During the War*
>
> *Round-headed nails (for boot heels), a hatchet, pudding, turkey, pickles, onions, pepper, paper, envelopes, socks, potatoes, chocolate, condensed milk, sugar, butter, sauce, towels, needles, thread, buttons, yarn, boiled ham, tea, cheese, cake, and books.*

How to Perform Fatigue Duty

Try carrying two buckets filled with water, one in each hand, back and forth to fill a container or water some plants. Carry some logs in for the fireplace. Stand in your front yard for a long time and listen to hear if anyone approaches by car or on foot, alerting your commanding officer if anyone looks suspicious. Clean and polish special trophies or mementos in your bedroom. If you don't enjoy doing these activities, you know how the Civil War soldiers felt about doing their similar chores!

How to Write a Letter Home

Write a letter to your folks telling them all about your experiences as a soldier, the things you are learning, and the new people you've met. Include a sketch of your camp and a black and white photo of yourself. If you do not have a black and white photograph, make a postcard-sized copy onto a buff or cream-colored sheet of paper. Trim the borders. You may want to write a brief note on the back.

A carte-de-visite framed for carrying.

and South taking photographs. Few people had enough money to own an expensive camera, so when a photographer came around, many soldiers would take advantage of the opportunity to have their "likeness" made. Some had pictures taken before going off to war in order to leave pictures of themselves behind for loved ones; others had photographs taken during the war to send to the folks back home. These postcard-like photos were called "carte-de-visite."

During the war, thousands of photographs were sent through the mail in both directions.

BASEBALL AND OTHER SPORTS

Civil War troops found many ways to amuse themselves. Outdoor sports were the event of choice when the weather was fine, and the soldiers competed in foot races, wrestling, boxing matches, football, and crick-

Regular Foodstuffs	War Era Substitutions:
Cows, pigs, chickens	frogs, snails, snakes
Coffee beans	toasted okra seeds, roasted acorns, dried sweet potatoes
Tea leaves	sumac berries, blackberry and raspberry leaves, sassafras roots
Milk	an egg white and a small lump of butter, beaten til frothy
Sugar	honey, sorghum, molasses, watermelon syrup
Flour	ground rice or cornmeal
Salt	boiled and skimmed dirt from the smokehouse floor or boiled seawater

Along with baseball, kickball was also a pastime of the soldiers.

et. Warmer weather also found the troops enjoying sack and wheelbarrow races, mock dress parades, and the more common pursuits of boating, fishing, or swimming. Baseball—also called round ball, town ball, or barn ball—was a favorite sport for many men who played as often as circumstances permitted.

Hundreds of rule books were distributed during the war, explaining the ins and outs of the game to many who were just learning how to play

this new national pastime. Yankee and Confederate baseball was a bit different from baseball in later years. Outfielders, called scouts, did not use gloves. Outs, or hands out, were achieved by either catching the ball out of the air or by hitting the player with a thrown ball. The pitcher stood on the pitcher's point while the striker, or batter, stood on the striker's point. Home plate was just that—a tin plate turned upside down. The ball was softer and larger, made out

Civil War Baseball Terms	Modern Baseball Terms
behind	catcher
club nine	team
foul tick	foul ball
match	game
muff	error
tally	score

rags tied around a walnut or a piece of cork. Bats were often improvised out of fence rails or barrel staves. The score was kept differently, with some games recording hits into the 40s and 50s. One Massachusetts regiment beat a New York unit with a score of 62 to 20.

One soldier wrote home telling of serious losses to their baseball team during a surprise attack at the second Battle of Bull Run: "Suddenly there was a scattering of fire, which three outfielders caught the brunt; the center field was hit and was captured, left and right field managed to get back to our lines. The attack … was repelled without serious difficulty, but we had lost not only our center field, but … the only baseball in Alexandria, Texas."[4]

GAMBLING AND GAMES

A favorite pastime for most soldiers involved any kind of game of chance or gambling, especially if there was an opportunity to multiply their greenbacks.

The parade ground has been a busy place for a week or so past, ball-playing having become a mania in camp. Officer and men forget, for a time, the differences in rank and indulge in the invigorating sport with a school boy's ardor.[3]

"Last Saturday a very exciting contest came off between two … horses, owned by two Brigadier Generals. Another match is announced for tomorrow and another for Saturday. With such examples, is it any wonder that gambling is on the increase? So far as my observation goes, nine men of every ten play cards for money.[5]

Card games, considered somewhat immoral at the time, were

Confederate dollar bills, aka greenbacks.

Union soldiers passing time by gambling.

sometimes forbidden by commanding officers. However, those commands were often ignored.

"The gambling urge of some Yanks was so strong that they would indulge in it at the risk of their lives as well as their fortunes. One group of poker zealots who found themselves a special target of Rebel gunners completed the hand, though swearing incessantly at the enemy for disturbing them, and then leisurely shifted to the unexposed side of a large tree to continue their play."[6]

The money soldiers won was used to buy much needed supplies. For those who had family in need the money was often sent home. (The soldiers usually played for money, but it was not uncommon for almost everyone to be out of cash. Then the soldiers would play for army rations or sutler's delicacies.) Many a soldier lost his entire next pay on unlucky wagers.

If there was a good snowfall in the winter months, everyone turned out for a rousing snowball fight. Troops fought against each other by regiments in mock battles with banners waving, drums beating out formations, and white missiles shooting through the air in place of bullets.

Despite orders to the contrary, many soldiers kept pets during the war. Dogs were the most common, but soldiers also kept cats, squirrels, and raccoons—one regiment from Wisconsin kept an eagle.

Soldiers also took advantage of opportunities for hunting game. The soldiers hunted a wide variety of animals, including raccoons, squirrels, opossums, and quail. Less often pursued were deer, wild ducks, wild hogs, and foxes. In areas near the coast, soldiers searched out mammoth turtles and their eggs. Rabbits presented opportunities for a good chase—hopefully with a good rabbit stew to follow.

Outdoor fun was always preferred, as the tents were stuffy, smelly, uncomfortably cramped quarters. But when the weather was poor the troops moved into their tents to play board games or cards. Sawed-off tree stumps were used as gaming tables for the men to set up checkers (commonly called draughts), chess, dominoes, or cribbage.

Relaxing with a friendly game of cards.

How to Make Your Own Civil War Board Game

You will need:
Paper
Colored pens
Scissors
Ruler
Dice
Buttons

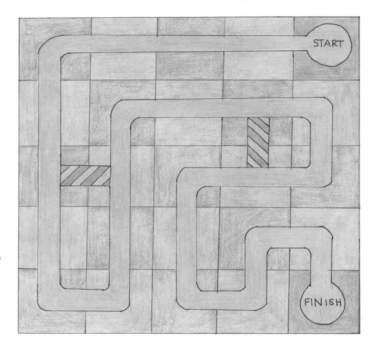

What kind of game would you like to play on a rainy afternoon? Take your paper, ruler, and pens and draw out a grid (see the illustration for an example). Decide on a path and use arrows to help players know where to go. Think of things that could have happened during the war that would send you back spaces (such as having to do guard duty, having your tent blown over, or being caught by the enemy) and forward spaces (such as leading your troops into battle, earning a commission, or picking up a fallen flag and carrying it forward into battle): fill in different spaces on your game board with these actions. Be sure to decorate your board. When you feel it is ready, round up your friends and sit down for an exciting Civil War experience. Use the buttons as your game pieces and roll the dice to move through the board—first one to the end wins!

DRINKING, SMOKING, AND SWAPPING

Drinking alcohol and smoking tobacco were very common in the army. The favored drinks were whisky, gin, beer, and wine. Soldiers had a hard time getting a hold of alcohol—either there was no place nearby to purchase it, or they didn't have enough money to buy what was available. During periods of quiet along the front battle lines, soldiers would often swap items of value, even though

Members of a Civil War band pose with their instruments displayed.

troops were generally forbidden from "trucking" or exchanging with the enemy.

Some Yanks and Rebs, shouting across the no-man's land between them, agreed to terms of exchange for goods. Others carried on trade by means of miniature boats sailed across rivers and streams. "On the Rappahannock [River] early in 1863 some New Jersey soldiers received a shipment 'by miniature boat six inches long' to which was attached the following note:

Gents U. S. Army
We wend you some tobacco by our Packet. Send us some coffee in return. Also a deck of cards if you have them, and we will send you more tobacco....[7]

MUSIC AND DRAMA

Music and singing were universal among the soldiers, whether in camp or on the march. In camp, soldiers often entertained themselves and others by playing musical instruments. Many regiments were authorized to form bands, and concerts were frequently given to entertain all the troops, officers and enlisted men alike. Smaller instruments were popular because they were portable and easy to play. Many soldiers brought instruments with them from home while others fashioned makeshift instruments out of whatever materials they could find.

The most common take-off was dress parade. At these sham affairs, officers and noncommissioned officers were sometimes required to march in the ranks while privates with exaggerated shoulder straps, improvised from orange peeling and even canteens, gave the commands.... Haversacks sometimes were replaced by tiny bags labeled "ten-days' rations.... "Officers" riding broken-down horses, candlesticks pinned on as medals and other ludicrous devices were introduced to add to the comic theme.[8]

Dixie's Land

Oh, Dixie, the land of King Cotton,
The home of the brave and the free;
A nation by freedom begotten,
The terror of despots to be.
Wherever thy banner is streaming,
Base tyranny quails at thy feet;
And liberty's sunlight is beaming
In splendor of majesty sweet.

Then three cheers for our Army so true,
Three cheers for our President too;
May our banner triumphantly wave
Over Dixie, the land of the brave!

When Liberty sounds her war rattle,
Demanding her right and her due,
The first land to rally to battle
Is Dixie, the home of the true.
Thick as leaves of the forest in summer,
Her brave sons will rise on each plain
And then strike till each vandal comer
Lies dead on the soil he would stain.

May the names of the dead that we cherish
Fill memory's cup to the brim;
May the laurels we've won never perish,
Nor our stars of their glory grow dim.
May our states of the South never sever
But companions of freedom e'er be;
May they flourish Confed'rate forever,
The boast of the brave and the free.

Common instruments were the harmonica, guitar, violin, spoons, jaw harp, flute or fife, and the drum.

Soldiers thoroughly enjoyed the dramatic arts. They put on regular performances, usually outdoors on rough stages built by the troops. Some of the plays performed were classics such as Shakespearean dramas; others were comedies, often mock dress parades written by the soldiers themselves. The soldiers very much enjoyed the shows that found humor in the difficulties of war, but their favorites were those that poked fun at their commanding officers, the "shoulder straps" (so called because of the insignia worn over the shoulders distinguishing them as officers).

FAVORITE CONFEDERATE SONGS

John Brown's Body
Dixie's Land
Goober Peas
God Save the South
Stonewall Jackson's Way
We Conquer or Die

READING

Reading was another way for the men to fill the long periods between campaigns. Some of the better-funded regiments established camp libraries that were housed in regimental "chapels" (actually tents or log cabins).

Most popular among the troops were the illustrated newspapers of Frank Leslie and Harper's Weekly, as well as the so-called dime novels—a quick and inexpensive read. All of these materials were usually available through the camp sutler. One soldier wrote home that he "longed more for something to read than for something to eat." [9]

Because Civil War soldiers came from all walks of life, many were well educated and could read Latin and Greek. Some soldiers studied Shakespeare (Hamlet and Macbeth were popular) and read from Milton's works (such as Paradise Lost); others could neither read nor write.

The Bible was immensely popular. The United States Christian Commission distributed tens of thousands of copies in the Union camps, and even more found their way into soldiers' hands—Northern and Southern alike—through family and friends.

Could You Have Been in a Civil War Band?

Purchase an inexpensive recorder with an instruction booklet at a music store. (It is easy to learn to play the recorder.) After you have learned how to play the notes, buy some sheet music for a popular Civil War tune and learn how to play it.

How to Read Like a Soldier

Choose a book that one of the soldiers might actually have read. Here is a short list to help you get started:

Tale of Two Cities, Great Expectations, or David Copperfield, by Charles Dickens

Any play by Shakespeare (look for a good children's version)

The Bible

A short, inexpensive novel written on some light-hearted topic (by any author)

Harper's Weekly was a favorite read among soldiers during the Civil War.

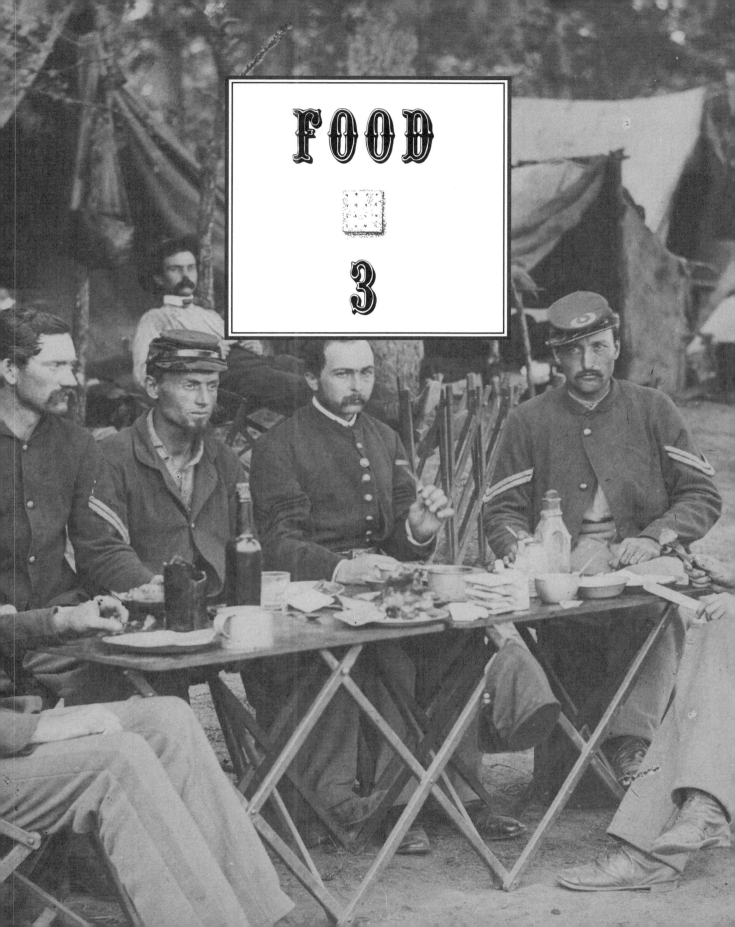

FOOD

3

Your stomach seems to rumble most of the time these days. A few months ago you and your men were issued full rations every few days. Beans simmered in pots over every campfire and there was meat enough for even the biggest eaters. Every morning the smell of freshly-brewed coffee hung in the sultry morning air. Then your regiment was relocated to the west, deep in the Appalachian Mountains. You are far from the nearest railroad—too far to receive food shipments with any regularity—and the mule-pulled supply trains have been cut off by an enemy advance down from the north. How things have changed—everyone seems to grumble most of the time these days!

FOOD SUPPLY

Soldiers in the Civil War obtained their food from many different sources. Throughout the war much of their food was provided by the Commissary Departments of either the Union or the Confederacy. These food supplies were fairly reliable and sometimes even plentiful. As the war continued and supplies became both more expensive and more difficult to obtain, the troops often supplemented their increasingly poor rations by foraging across the countryside, purchasing from sutlers (civilians, licensed by the military commander, who sold various provisions to soldiers in the field or in camp), or having foodstuffs sent from home.

THE COMMISSARY DEPARTMENT

The Commissary Department had the job of buying food for the armies, storing it, and getting it to the troops wherever they were. This job was easier for the Northern army since they already had a Commissary Department in place before the war started. Both the North and South had well-developed farm economies, but the widespread destruction of farmland in the South as the war progressed made conditions worse for the Southern troops.

RATIONS

A ration is the amount of food authorized for one soldier for one day. Rations can be issued daily, weekly or monthly or—if food was scarce—partially or even not at all!

Soldiers were sometimes issued desiccated vegetables, which were small, square cakes formed of dehydrated vegetables. To prepare, they were simply put in a pot of water

A commissary supply line sends out supplies.

and boiled. These were so distasteful to the soldiers that they called them "desecrated vegetables."

Rations were distributed uncooked, so it was up to the soldiers to figure out how to prepare their meals. Some gathered together to share and cook rations in a group they called a "mess": they called each other "messmates." Others preferred to cook and eat their meals alone. Each soldier carried his food in a haversack (if he had one), a canvas bag with a strap to go over the shoulder, or else wrapped in a square of cloth.

As the army issued few cooking utensils beyond a kettle and a mess plate, soldiers had to come up with their own utensils, pots, and pans.

US Army Commissary Rations
3 August 1861 through 20 June 1864

To every individual:
meat:
  12 ounces pork or bacon, or
  1 pound 4 ounces salt or fresh beef
bread:
  1 pound 6 ounces soft bread or flour, or
  1 pound hard bread, or
  1 pound 4 ounces cornmeal

To every 100 rations:
  30 pounds potatoes, when practicable,
  & 1 quart molasses
  15 pounds beans or peas, and
  10 pounds rice or hominy
  10 pounds green [unroasted] coffee, or
  8 pounds roasted coffee, or
  1 pound 8 ounces tea
  15 pounds sugar
  4 quarts vinegar
  1 pound 4 ounces star candles
  4 pounds soap
  3 pounds 12 ounces salt
  4 ounces pepper

How to Sew a Haversack

You will need:

1 yard of plain canvas
Thread
A 1-yard strip of webbing
Sewing machine
Scissors

Fold the canvas in half (wrong side out) and trim off sides until the sack is as wide as you would like it to be. The sack should be large enough to hold all your food, but not so large that you can't carry it comfortably while marching. Unfold the sack and press the top and bottom edges over 1/4 inch onto the wrong side of the fabric. Sew the edges (not together) so that you end up with two finished edges. Then re-fold the sack, still wrong side out, so that the two finished edges meet at the top to become the opening for the haversack. Sew up the sides of the sack using 1/4 inch seams. Measure the webbing against your body to determine how much of it to use for the strap (if you want the haversack to hang lower use more webbing, higher, use less). Sew the webbing to the inside of the haversack to make a strap. Turn everything right side out and fill up your haversack with provisions!

Step 1

Step 2

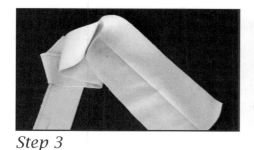

Step 3

Step 4

Once your haversack is finished you can use it to carry your lunch on your next campaign!

How to Make a Civil War Cooking Pot

You will need:
  Clean, empty coffee can
  1 large nail
  12—15 inches heavy wire
  Pliers

Using the nail, poke two holes opposite each other 1 inch below the rim of the can. Insert ends of wire into each of the holes to form a handle, twisting wire ends with pliers to secure. To get cooking, hang your cooking pot by its handle over a fire. Or place the pot itself into coals and use the handle to take it out (use hot pads and be careful—the pot will be hot).

Familiar Canned Foods Available During the Civil War

Tabasco Sauce
Lea and Perrins Worcestershire Sauce
Borden's Condensed Milk
VanCamp's Pork and Beans

THE FOUR BASIC RATIONS

During the Civil War, food could not be preserved or stored as well as it is today, so the troops did not have very much variety in their diet. Canned foods had been newly created and were not yet in widespread use.

Basic rations for both the Northern and Southern armies were the same: meat, hard bread (called hardtack), beans, and coffee.

MEAT

Larger sections of the army were often accompanied by herds of cows and/or pigs in order to more easily provide the large quantity of beef or pork necessary to feed the troops. Where this was not possible (which was far too often for the soldiers' liking), soldiers were issued salted meat or, in some instances, dried jerky.

HARDTACK

Hardtack was a biscuit made of flour, water, and a few other ingredients. When eaten fresh, the hard bread was palatable to most soldiers. However, most hardtack didn't get to the troops for months, and by the time it did it was so hard that soldiers couldn't even bite it. The soldiers nicknamed the crackers "toothdullers" or "sheet iron crackers," and told jokes and stories about them. Soldiers even wrote songs and poems about this daily fare.

'Tis the song that is uttered in camp by night and day,
'Tis the wail that is mingled with each snore;
'Tis the sighing of the soul for spring chickens far away,
"Oh hard crackers, come again not more!"

'Tis the song of the soldier, weary, hungry and faint,
Hard crackers, hard crackers, come again no more;
Many days have I chewed you and uttered no complaint,
Hard crackers, hard crackers, come again no more!"

—from a soldiers' parable called "Hard Times"

Hardtack was often stored and transported in open wooden crates. Exposed to the elements, it could become damp from rain, growing a thin covering of green mold, or become infested with weevils, small bugs that ate their way through the crackers. The soldier called these older, tunnel-ridden crackers "wormcastles." However unappetizing the hardtack might be, sometimes it was the only food available to the soldiers, so they came up with numerous ways to make the hardtack edible. Some soldiers, after scraping off the outer layer of mold, would then toast the crackers over a fire to drive out the weevils. Others would soak their hardtack in a pot of hot coffee, skimming off the bugs as they floated to the top.

There were as many different and creative ways to prepare hardtack as one could think of, but perhaps the most common was to soak the hardtack in water or coffee, and then fry it in beef or pork fat. The soldiers called this "skillygalee." Another favorite recipe of Confederate soldiers, using cornmeal, which was common in their rations, was "coosh." This dish was made by frying up some bacon in a pan and then adding boiling water and cornmeal to make a thick, brownish gravy.

BEANS

The beans the army issued were usually dry navy beans rather than canned beans. These had to be soaked in water and then cooked for many hours. If the soldiers were not

---

The Army Bean

There's a spot that the soldiers all love,
The mess-tent's the place that we mean,
And the dish we best like to see there
Is the old-fashioned, white Army Bean
Chorus
'Tis the bean that we mean,
And we'll eat as we ne'er ate before;
The Army Bean, nice and clean,
We'll stick to our beans evermore.
Now the bean, in its primitive state,
Is a plant we have all often met;
And when cooked in the old army style
It has charms we can never forget.
Chorus

---

on a march they could put them in a pot with some salt pork and molasses, then bury the pot in their campfire ashes to cook overnight. Meat and beans was a common and popular dish. The soldiers ate them so often, and liked them so well, that they wrote many songs about them.

Civil War Recipe for Soldiers' Beans

Take as many beans as you want for a mess and ... partly boil them then take a spade and dig a hole large aneugh [sic] for the pot you are going to cook the beans in and build a fire in it and get it as warm as you can, then take the pot of beans and put a piece of meat in the center of the pot then cover the pot over and put it in the hole covering the pot with the coals that are in the hole and shovel earth on top of them and in twenty-four hours you have a soldier's dish of baked beans.[1]

COFFEE

Coffee was very important to the soldiers, but as the war progressed it was increasingly difficult to obtain. (Soldiers much preferred it to tea.) There is no record of what type of coffee was issued to the troops, but as the war went on all coffee became scarce, especially in the South. Soldiers tried many substitutes, including roasted corn, rye, acorns, cotton seed, chinquapin (a nut), sorghum (a type of grain like wheat or rye), and chicory root (a plant something like a dandelion), all without much satisfaction.

Recipe for Dried Meat

1 1/2 to 2 pounds beef brisket
1/2 teaspoon pepper
1 teaspoon garlic salt
1 teaspoon onion powder
4 tablespoon Worcestershire sauce
2 teaspoon Liquid Smoke

Trim visible fat off brisket and slice very thin, 1/8 inch. Combine all other ingredients in a glass dish and mix well. Add meat, marinate overnight. Lay beef strips on oven rack with a cookie sheet set below to catch drippings. Bake in a 200 degree oven for 5–8 hours until dry but not brittle.

Dried meat for your haversack!

Recipe for Hardtack

2 cups all-purpose flour
1/2 to 3/4 cups water
1–2 tablespoon Crisco or vegetable fat
1/2 teaspoon salt

Mix the ingredients into a stiff batter, knead several times, and roll out to 1/2 inch thickness on well-greased cookie sheet. Bake 25–30 minutes at 350 degrees, then remove from oven and cut into pieces about 3 inches by 3 inches. Punch four rows of holes in each cracker, four holes each row, then turn the crackers over and bake another 25–30 minutes at 350 degrees.

After the hardtack is baked, cut it into cracker-sized pieces with a knife and then serve it up to your troops!

Recipe for Baked Beans

1 onion
2 tablespoon vegetable oil
1 12-ounce package dry navy beans
2 ham hocks
1/2 cup molasses
1 tablespoon cider vinegar
salt and pepper to taste

Chop the onion and fry in the oil. In an ovenproof pot with lid, place the onions, beans, ham hocks, molasses, and vinegar. Add water to cover. Bake 6–8 hours, or until beans are tender, checking periodically to add water if beans become dry. When done, remove meat from ham hocks and discard bones. Stir meat into beans. Salt and pepper to taste.

How to Make Coffee From Acorns

Acorns are edible after the tannin is leached or boiled out. Collect acorns from areas you know have not been treated with pesticides.* Harvest season is in the fall, from September to October. Collect only brown acorns, avoiding those with a greenish cast.

You will need:
Acorns
Stove
Pot
Water
Oven
Cookie sheet

To prepare the acorns, wash them with warm water (do not use soap) and remove the nuts from the shells. Chop the nut meat and boil 15−30 minutes until the water turns brown. Rinse and repeat until water is clear. Roast the acorns by placing the chopped meats on a cookie sheet in a 250-degree oven and cook until brittle. When cool, grind the nuts and boil as for coffee.

*Red oak acorns tend to be bitter; white oak acorns (recommended) are sweeter.[2]

FORAGING

As they traveled or camped, Confederate and Union soldiers sometimes took for themselves whatever crops or animals they could find, even though foraging was often forbidden by commanding officers. Nothing was sacred to a forager, especially in enemy territory. He lifted carrots, potatoes, or other crops right out of a family garden. He raided the henhouse. (If he was lucky enough to find eggs, he might roast them in the coals of his fire overnight, taking them along in his pocket to eat during a march the next day.) If a home was abandoned he would go through the kitchen looking for any staples that might have been left behind such as honey, sugar, or molasses. He would search a barn for oats, corn, or even farm animals. A group of Confederate soldiers, "specifically ordered not to take farmers' hogs, simply decided to call the hogs bears instead, and then gleefully boasted of the abundance of wild 'bears' they shot and ate on the march."[3]

As the war went on, most soldiers were reduced to a breakfast of hardtack and tea or coffee, then a dinner or supper of whatever they could obtain for themselves. "'On more than one occasion,' wrote Colonel Arthur Markham of the Atlanta Calvary Brigade, 'our soup had nothing more in it than oats we had stolen from the horses and grass that we had picked in the fields.'" Percival Lyons, a doctor with a once well-fed infantry, wrote to his wife that "for more than a week our lunches and dinners have consisted of a thin soup made with whatever wild vegetables we could find."[4] For one young soldier, food became so scarce that he wrote home to his family, "I often wish I had to eat what Aunt Polly's dog gets and what you throw away."

How to Eat Like a Civil War Soldier

Rations have been issued and it is time to set off on a march. What will you pack in your haversack before you head out?

Hardtack (recipe above)
A tin of baked beans
Sliced carrots
Jam
Nuts and/or dried fruit
Dried meat
A canteen, filled with water (for making coffee or tea)

Watch out for weevils! These common pests often ate their way through the contents of a soldier's haversack. Hungry soldiers still ate what was left.

BATTLE

4

The whole reason you joined the army was to fight. Now—finally—the day of battle is upon you. The fife and drum sounds the reveille and soldiers hastily tumble out of beds and tents. Small fires spring up in the chilly, gray air as the soldiers start to brew their bitter coffee. The older soldiers start emptying their haversacks: this morning they will cook and eat all the rations they have, as it might be two or three days before anyone has a chance to eat again. Better to go into battle with a full stomach and an empty haversack—who knows but that this meal might be your last? The drums sound again signaling time to break camp and start the march to the battlefield.

LIGHTENING THE LOAD

A soldier had to carry everything he needed on his back. The longer a soldier was in the service, the more things he found he could make do without. By the end of his enlistment period, a soldier carried only the barest of essentials. Often all he would carry inside his haversack or rolled in the oilcloth was a change of socks, writing paper, stamps and envelopes, ink and pen, razor, toothbrush, comb and other personal items. One highly prized item that a soldier would try to keep was the oilcloth or gum blanket, which could be used as a ground cover, a waterproof poncho, or a makeshift tent. The average Civil War soldier carried about 50 pounds of equipment and clothing.

MILITARY STRATEGY

The battlefield was a place of action, but almost always that action had been preceded by extensive planning. Generals and other superior officers spent countless hours engaged in

Basic Principles of Military Strategy

1. The objective (goal to be accomplished)
2. Offense (method and plan of attack)
3. Cooperation (troops working together)
4. Concentration (large numbers of troops massed in strategic locations)
5. Economy (using a smaller effort for a greater benefit)
6. Maneuver (movement of troops at various times and locations)
7. Surprise (keeping the enemy unaware of presence)
8. Security (being sure of position and forces; not vulnerable)
9. Simplicity (avoiding complicated maneuvers)

analysis and discussion regarding principles of military strategy. Strategy in the military could be boiled down to a list of basic principles that needed to be addressed when planning a campaign.

Civil War generals had differing philosophies regarding military strategy. Some felt very strongly that sticking to basic principles such as those on the previous page would guarantee victory; others felt that war was unpredictable and that a general needed to be flexible when formulating a strategy. General Nathan Bedford Forrest had perhaps the simplest strategy of all: "get there firstest with the mostest."[1]

Generals worked hard to plan all aspects of their campaigns. In a time when a good map could spell the difference between victory and defeat, they were careful to obtain as much information as possible about the topography of a potential battlefield. In enemy territory, sometimes the best they could do was a quick sketch drawn from horseback by a reconnaissance soldier, but if they had the luxury of time and perhaps a map maker for hire, they could get a detailed drawing of the field.

ENTERING THE FRAY

As your regiment approaches the battlefield the din is tremendous. You can see the most intense areas of fighting by the clouds of smoke that hang

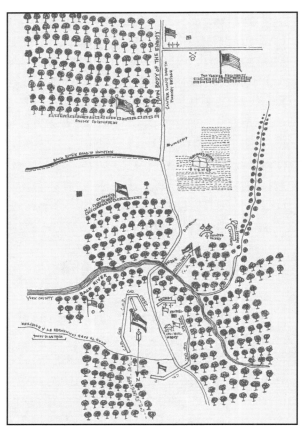

Sketch of the Battle of Bethel.

in the air above the trees. Suddenly the drums sound an alarm. The Major at the head of your marching column shouts out the orders: "Attention, company!" As the command echoes down the line, your soldiers fall into their places. The fife and drum beat out their signals, and soon everyone has loaded his weapon and is prepared to fire—just as you have practiced in those endless drills back at camp. Your thoughts wander momentarily to home, family, and God, but you are jarred back to the present by a cannonball's impact in the field ahead of you, and the sudden sizzle of hot shrapnel in the air.

The battlefield was the test for every military man. On that day, all else was left behind and forgotten: the boredom of camp, the cold nights, even the homesickness. Although the thought of fighting was often on a soldier's mind, active battle consumed a relatively small portion of the soldier's actual enlistment time. When the time to fight actually arrived, almost every soldier was afraid. Some were afraid of being wounded, others were afraid of showing cowardice.

When the order came to advance, the men moved forward in tight formation, thirteen inches from the man in the front line to the man in the next line or rank, and touching elbows with the men on either side. If any man ran, his leaders usually had orders to shoot him.

Sometimes after all the rush of marching to the battlefield and getting into formation, there were tense moments of waiting for the "opening of the ball"—the first gunshots of the actual battle.

Once things had gotten underway, some soldiers discovered that rather than being fearful, they were filled with new and different feelings: sometimes courage, sometimes excitement, sometimes rage.

LINES OF SUPPLY

An essential part of moving troops to battlefields was maintain-

We lay there about eight minutes and yet it seemed an age to me, for showers of bullets and grape [shot] were passing over me ... and not allowed to fire a single shot.... Oh how my heart palpitated! It seemed to thump the ground (I lay on my face) as hard as the enemy's bullets. The sweat from off my face run in a stream from the tip ends of my whiskers.... Twice I exclaimed aloud ... My God, why don't they order us to charge?"[12]

Make Your Own Rebel Yell

When the Confederate soldiers were told to charge in battle, they let out a yell to tell the Union soldiers they meant business. One of the soldiers of the 9th Virginia Cavalry described the yell as "Who-who-ey! Who-ey! Who-ey!" all in short, high bursts like a dog's yip. If you were a soldier, what would your battle cry be?

ing the lines of supply. Because the troops required many supplies, major military operations had to be kept to areas with rail and water lines, or with significant and secure roadways. Both the North and the South had several rail routes that ran east-west, and the South had several that ran north-south. The North had the advantage on the seas and was able to successfully blockade significant Southern ports, thereby shutting down trade as well as foreign aid from overseas. However, there were some features in the Southern states that gave them distinct advantages. Key among these were numerous rivers in Virginia that ran perpendicular to the direct line of advance, allowing for relatively easy movement of troops and supplies; several sheltered mountain valleys that led from Virginia and West Virginia directly north to Pennsylvania; and the Shenandoah valley, which provided a safe approach to Washington from the rear. (This last approach was put to good use by Generals Lee, Jackson, and Early.)

Soldiers work on repairing the railroad to keep the supply lines open.

How to Plan Your Own Battle Campaign

Review the 9 principles of military strategy on p. 33. Ask as many questions about what might happen during your campaign as you can think of. What are the possibilities, risks, exposures, and strengths? Send out scouts or even spies if you cannot gather all the information yourself. Once you have gotten all the information you can, make a list on your paper with two columns, dividing your information up by whether it is a strength or a weakness, an asset or a liability, a positive or a negative. Draw a sketch of the battlefield with all important structures and geographical elements. Then you will need to do what a general does: think hard, and then make decisions. Deciding can be the hardest part, because even with excellent planning, things can still go wrong—sometimes terribly wrong—and men can lose their lives. On the other hand, if you don't take any chances, you will never win the war.

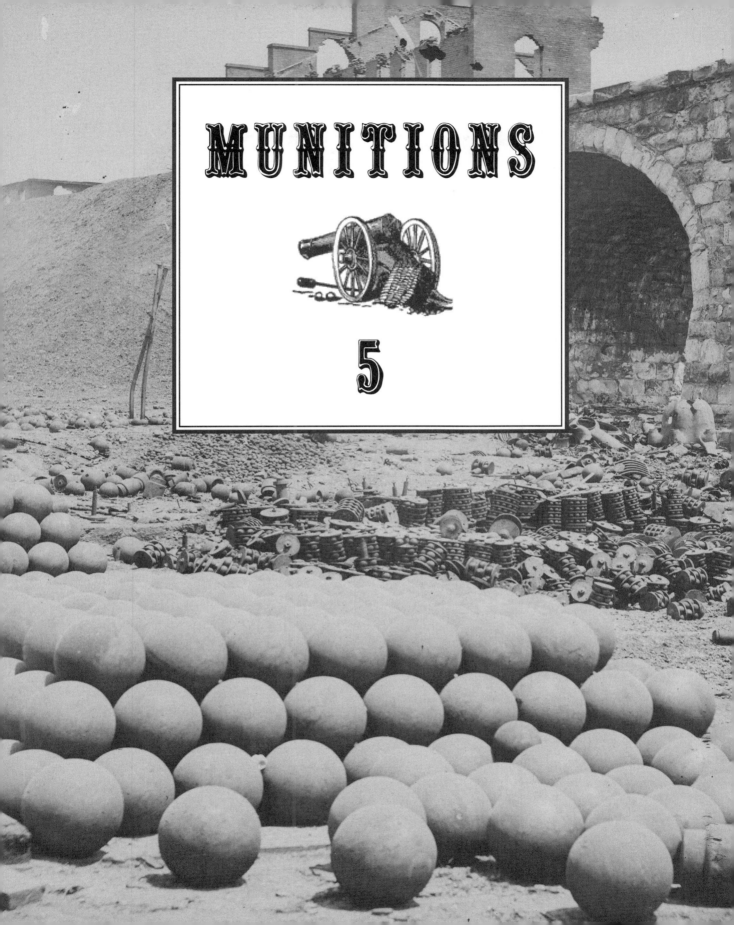

MUNITIONS

5

A soldier without a gun isn't much good to anyone—neither is a gun without any bullets. You are weary of the constant struggle to get enough of both. Of the men who have guns, many brought those weapons from home. They have long since run out of ammunition, and your repeated requests for the necessary ball and cartridge sizes have gone unanswered. You've been able to capture some rifles, ammunition, and powder from the Union troops you fought last week, but you can only hope that will be enough to hold you until the supply lines open up again.

SUPPLYING MUNITIONS

Civil War soldiers used two types of firearms: small arms (guns) and artillery (cannons). At the outset of the war neither the North nor the South had enough small arms or artillery to supply their soldiers with weapons. The governments of both sides bought weapons from Europe while they waited for American armories to gear up for war production. Most of the imported small arms came from England, France, Germany, Austria, and Belgium, but the soldiers disliked them because they were heavy and unreliable (the average rifle weighed 8 or 9 pounds), so the soldiers nicknamed them "pumpkin slingers" (using .69-caliber bullets, they fired the largest ammunition of all shoulder arms) or "mules" (they could "kick further than they [could] shoot").[1]

Eventually both the North and the South supplied their troops with two rifles that were very popular among the soldiers: the British-manufactured Enfield, and the American-made Springfield rifles. Even though these were widely issued, the soldiers still needed to use so many of their own weapons that all of the Enfields and Smithfields combined made up less than 40 percent of all the shoulder arms used by both the North and the South.[3] Although bayonets were initially issued, soldiers rarely used them for their intended purpose. Swords, sabers, and other weapons were also popular, but most fatalities were caused by firearms.

A Springfield rifle.

SMALL ARMS

Small arms included muskets (smooth-bore, long-barreled guns), rifles (shoulder guns with spiral grooves on the inside of the barrel), carbines (short-barreled muskets or rifles), and handguns (pistols and re-volvers). When a weapon was "rifled," spiral grooves were cut into the in-side of the barrel to spin the bullet as it was shot. Smooth-bore rifles had no grooves.

Those who owned guns and knew how to use them usually brought their own weapons to war with them. Officers often found themselves with groups of men armed with anything from double-barreled shotguns, flint-locks, and muzzle-loaders to small handguns and breechloaders.

Double-barreled shotgun—a long gun with two barrels that were able to discharge either at the same time or separately.

Flintlock—a long gun that used a firing mechanism to strike flint against steel, sending the spark into a small pan filled with gunpowder.

Muzzle-loader—a long gun that was loaded by ramming the bullet, gunpowder and wadding down the open end of the muzzle, front-loading.

Breechloader—a long gun that was loaded at the breech (in back of the barrel), rear-load-ing.

Handguns—lightweight, small-er guns with a short barrel, breech loading.

Breech-loaders, invented around 1800, came into wider use during the Civil War. They had many advantages over muzzle-loaders: soldiers could reload faster, had less exposure to enemy fire, and required less space to move around in while reloading. They were also much easier to reload for the cavalry who were on horse-back and often moving at top speeds. But both armies were slow to adopt the new breech-loaders because they were more expensive and required more parts than the older guns.

The Confederacy was not as well equipped as the Union, and the Rebels sought to capture as many enemy guns (and cartridges) as pos-sible. Southern soldiers coveted the North's Spencer carbines, Sharp's

> *I think the Johnnies [rebels] are getting rattled.... They are afraid of our repeating rifles. They say we are not fair, that we have guns that we load up on Sunday and shoot all the rest of the week. This I know, I feel a good deal more confidence in myself with a 16 shooter in my hands than I used to with a single shot rifle.*[4]

rifles, and especially the Henry rifle, a lever-action repeater that could fire sixteen .44 caliber bullets as fast as the soldier could pull the lever.

Because the volunteer soldiers came from all kinds of different backgrounds, a single company contained both experienced marksmen as well as soldiers who had never so much as held a gun. These new soldiers had to be taught everything about their weapons: care and cleaning, proper handling, loading, and shooting. They also needed repeated drilling to enable them to aim, discharge, and reload very quickly, and they needed to be ready to perform these duties without hesitation when they were in the heat of battle under enemy fire.

ARTILLERY

All firearms larger than small arms were known as artillery or cannon. The artillery was the smallest branch of the military for both the North and the South. There were dozens of different types of cannon used during the Civil War, but they could all be identified as either smoothbore or rifled, and as either muzzle or breech loading. These basic types could be further categorized by other criteria.

The "Napoleon" cannon was widely used by both sides during the war. A smooth bore weapon, it had a range of 2,000 yards.

The cannons were accompanied by caissons or limbers (basically

---

How to Categorize Cannon

Weight of projectile	*Caliber (diameter)*	*Inventor or factory where made*
12-pounder	*3-inch*	*Parrott*
24-pounder	*8-inch*	*Napoleon*
32-pounder	*10-inch*	*Dahlgren*
		Rodman

A group of soldiers poses in front of a loaded caisson; other caissons stand in the background.

A Napoleon cannon.

an ammunition chest on wheels). Hitched together, a caisson and a cannon were together pulled by a team of six horses.

A standard field artillery battery consisted of six guns with their crews. The Confederacy artillery batteries often had to wait months to become fully equipped. Sometimes they had to wait for their cannon to be manufactured and shipped. Sometimes they had to wait for their ammunition. Sometimes they had to wait for the horses they needed in order to move their heavy equipment. While they waited, the officers divided their troops into gunners and drivers and drilled them in their duties.

A sergeant or corporal stood at the rear to oversee the process and to sight the piece. Repeated drilling ensured that each gunner knew his

movements and could perform them with precision, even without verbal commands, which would have been inaudible during battle. Well trained gun crews could fire off two rounds in sixty seconds.

SMALL ARMS MUNITIONS AND ORDNANCE

The war created a need for millions of different cartridges for an enormous variety of weapons. It was extremely difficult for the ordnance (artillery) officers to supply all the different types of ammunition the soldiers needed because each kind of gun required its own size (caliber or gauge) of bullets. In 1863, the Union Army officially recognized 121 different types of guns—and all of these needed to be appropriately supplied with powder and ammunition by the ordnance officers. The Confederacy

recognized weapons of any kind, but shared the challenge of obtaining ammunition. If an opportunity presented itself to capture ammunition in addition to weapons, the soldiers took full advantage of it. If the bullet supply ran out, Confederate soldiers resorted to making their own from bullet molds, or, if those weren't available, by using more creative methods.

One type of bullet, the minnie ball, was a small, hollow, conical bullet made of soft lead. About 1/2 inch in size, it was invented by French army Captain Claude F. Minnie. After the gun was fired, the base of the shot expanded so that it fit tightly,

instead of "bouncing" off the sides of the barrel as it traveled along. This tight fit, along with the rifling along the barrel, increased both the range and the accuracy of the gun.

The range of a smooth-bore shoulder arm is about 300 feet. A rifle-bore has a range of 750 to 900 feet. The smoothbores were extremely inaccurate except at very close range, so Southerners frequently turned them into something like a shotgun by loading them with what they called "buck and ball," which was three smaller shots loaded behind a regular full-sized ball.

A Confederate artillery yard.

ARTILLERY MUNITIONS

Artillery ammunition included solid shot, canister, shell, and grape shot. These shots came in different calibers. Solid shot was used for long-range, fixed targets. Canister, shell, and grape shot all consisted of smaller scattershot combined with gunpowder into one projectile, some wrapped in cloth or canvas (looking like a cluster of grapes), others encased in a tin can.

Some Missouri Rebels actually used sewing thimbles as molds when they poured their lead, poking a pointed stick into the still liquid metal as it cooled to give it a hollow base. "This gave the bullet the form of a minnie ball which just fitted our guns," wrote one of the Missouri boys, "and we could shoot through a boxcar 300 yards away."[6]

Solid shot.

Canister shot.

Grape shot.

A buck and ball cartridge.

Two different types of minnies.

How to Prepare & Fire Cannon–Drill for Gunner Artillerymen

Gunner 1*: hand a cartridge (of ball and powder combined) to gunner 2

Gunner 2: place cartridge into muzzle of cannon

Gunner 3: shove cartridge down the muzzle to bottom with a rammer

Gunner 4: poke through the vent hole at the breech (using a wire pick) and rip open the cloth bag of powder at base of cartridge exposing the black powder

Gunner 5: place a primer (attached to a braided cord) over the vent hole and jerk the lanyard to spark the powder and discharge the cannon

Gunner 6: ram the barrel with a soaked sponge to extinguish any burning embers (to avoid igniting the powder of the next cartridge)

Gunner 1: start the process again

*official gunner numbers may differ

How to Make a Marshmallow Gun

What you need:

About 5 ½ feet PVC pipe
2 PVC tee connectors
1 PVC coupling piece
2 PVC end caps
Spray paint
Mini Marshmallows

1. Cut your PVC pipe however long you want the barrel.

2. Cut the barrel into three pieces. Two of the pieces with be short, and one will be longer.

3. Connect the pieces with the two tee connectors, putting the two shorter pieces next to each other. This will be the end near your mouth. Place the coupling piece on the end for the mouthpiece. (Optional: Place another coupling piece on the end if you like.)

4. Cut two pieces for the handles. Put the end caps on the bottom.

5. Put the handles in the tee connectors.

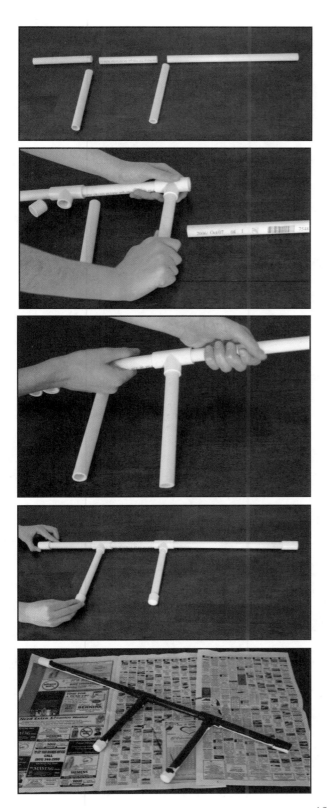

49

DISCIPLINE

6

It is more difficult than you imagined to keep a company of tired, hungry, disgruntled men in order. Yesterday two men got into a fight. Today one man refused to complete his assigned fatigue duty. Another fell asleep on his watch last night—and this was a childhood friend who enlisted especially to be in your company under your command. Someone has to discipline these troops, and although some of it can be delegated to the provost marshal, there are some decisions that can only be made by you. The day dawned perfect and spring-like, but your heart takes no joy in the beauty that surrounds you, knowing the unpleasant tasks that lie ahead.

MILITARY DISCIPLINE

It was no easy task to discipline the troops. Although soldiers were generally willing to obey their professional commanders—usually military school graduates who spoke with the authority of years of training—they weren't as willing to obey the friends or relatives who had recently been given commissions to head volunteer regiments. Military discipline generally used shame and pain to maintain order, at least for lesser offenses. The Provost Marshal of the army was responsible for enforcing military rules, but the punishments for lesser crimes were sometimes handed out by the military officers themselves, often on the spot.

The most serious crimes received the harshest punishments and could be ordered only by a court martial (a select board of 3 or more officers).

Only two authorities could pardon a soldier of his crime: the commanding general or the Confederate States President. Neither Union nor Confederate services dictated exact punishments for every possible crime. Instead, commanding officers could generally decide what punishments to hand down for a soldier's crimes. Military courts

A provost marshal.

51

weren't always able to be convened to decide upon punishments because they took time and attention away from more urgent matters such as fighting a battle.

PETTY OFFENCES

Crime:

Not doing camp duties, such as keeping equipment in good working order.

Possible punishment (Often involved doing extra labor):

Extra camp duties, such as chopping wood, fetching water, or digging latrines.

MODERATE OFFENCES

Crime:

Straggling, minor cowardice, drunkenness, theft, desertion, bounty jumping (taking money for enlistment, but then deserting), malingering (pretending illness), and insubordination (not obeying a commanding officer).

Possible Punishment (Often involved social embarrassment):

Extra fatigue duty, extra guard duty, reduction in rank, and public humiliations such as "riding the wooden mule" (sitting atop a narrow rail set up high enough that a soldier's feet couldn't touch the ground), being "bucked and gagged," (sitting with knees drawn in to chin, arms hugging legs, hands tied and a rag stuffed in the mouth), being tied up by the thumbs, or doing barrel drill (either wearing a barrel instead of clothing, or being made to balance, standing, atop a barrel, usually holding a sign labeling one's crime). Punishments usually lasted several hours.

SERIOUS OFFENCES

Crime:

Desertion, major cowardice, serious theft, sleeping on guard duty, trading with the enemy, spying, and murder.

Possible Punishment:

Sentenced to military prison, branding (either on the face or the hip), being drummed out of camp (being forced to publicly leave camp in disgrace to the beat of a drum), and execution by firing squad or by hanging. (Flogging had been outlawed several years before the war.)

Riding the wooden mule.

Blanket toss.

Barrel drill.

Sketch of a firing squad performing an execution of five deserters.

Why do you think punishments during the Civil War were so harsh? Part of the reason was that many men's lives were at stake. For example, if someone fell asleep on guard duty, a large number of soldiers could be ambushed and killed. Another reason was that if men did not obey their commanding officer, the troops lost the strength of working as a unified force, leaving themselves weaker and more vulnerable to the enemy.

How to Discipline Your Troops

What punishments would you use to discipline your own troops? Write a list of the different "crimes" that are committed in your group. Talk with your troops to decide what punishments would be appropriate for the various violations of your rules. Make a poster-sized list and put it up near your camp. If you like, appoint a provost marshal to manage disciplinary matters for you.

Assigning a provost marshal may help keep your troops in order.

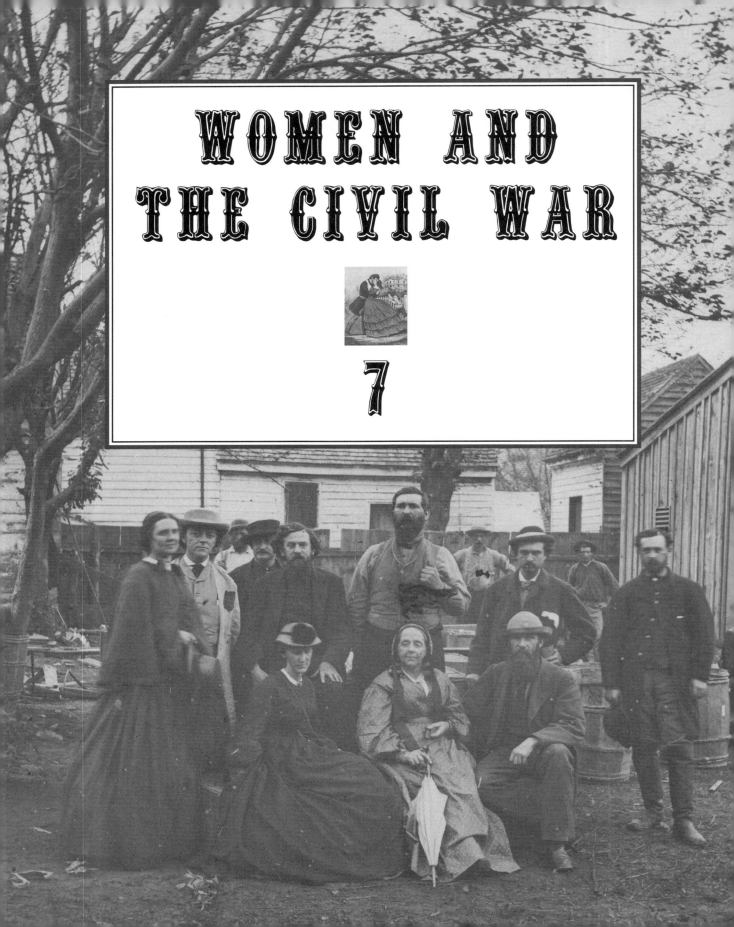

WOMEN AND THE CIVIL WAR

7

One day a small group of women arrive in camp. They are from the Ladies War Aid Society, and they come with baskets of bread, jam, and other delicacies—delicious food you haven't tasted in a long time! Some of your men who were injured in battle have been taken from the battlefield to a nearby general hospital. There they are treated by nurses, often other members of the Ladies War Aid Society, who administer medicine, cleanse and treat wounds, and read and write letters for the soldiers.

WAR AND WOMEN

Women were a significant part of the Civil War. Some saw the war as an opportunity to lead the fight for the abolition of slavery and the equality of women. Others used their roles in the family and community to provide support for soldiers in the field. Forming organized groups with names such as the Ladies Aid Society, these women gathered together to knit, sew, bake, write letters for, and even exert political influence on behalf of the soldiers. Still other women served directly in the camps and battlefields as soldiers, spies, doctors, and nurses.

ABOLITIONISTS AND SUFFRAGISTS

Elizabeth Cady Stanton and Susan B. Anthony were organizers of the National Women's Loyalty League. As part of this group they called for a constitutional amendment to end slavery. They argued that men and women should receive equal pay for equal work and that women

Susan B. Anthony

should be allowed to vote. They also argued that women, not just men, should be allowed to be field nurses during the Civil War.

LADIES' RELIEF AND AID SOCIETIES

The Women's Volunteer Aid Society of Munroe, Georgia, was one of many war relief societies formed during the war. They cooked and sewed, donating what they could to help the war effort. With fabric selling for 25 dollars per yard, Southern women sometimes tore apart old mattresses and used the fibers to make homespun fabric. They also cut up old carpets to sew into blankets for the troops to use during the cold winter months.

SOLDIERS, SPIES, DOCTORS, AND NURSES

Susie Baker, born a slave, married Sergeant Edward King and was appointed laundress of his regiment, the 33rd U.S. Colored Troops 1st South Carolina Volunteers. Even though she was only fourteen years old at the time, she taught the entire black regiment to read and write—they taught her how to shoot a gun. Eventually she became a nurse and helped organize a branch of the Woman's Relief Corps.

During the Civil War, Dr. Mary Walker volunteered as a surgeon in the Union Army after the Army refused to give her a commission. She worked both in the hospitals and as a field surgeon. Dr. Walker was the first female surgeon to serve in the Army. Although she served the Union cause, she would often cross into Confederate territory to treat wounded civilians. She also acted as a spy, and was a prisoner of war. In 1865 she was awarded a Congressional Medal of Honor for her Civil War service. She was the only woman vetran to earn this honor.

Dr. Mary Walker in her later years.

Jennie Hodges served and fought for three years under the alias of Albert Cashier. During her service she fought about forty battles and skirmishes. Even when she became extrememly ill and was in danger of being discovered by the doctor, she managed to persuade him to work with her as an out patient (so she wouldn't be seen in his office). Her identity as a woman was not revealed until 1913.

Clara Barton, "Angel of the Battlefield," worked tirelessly as a nurse

Clara Barton.

throughout the war. Often braving gunfire, she provided for the immediate needs of the wounded and dying. After the war, Clara Barton established the American Red Cross.

In this sketch, a civil war nurse comforts a wounded soldier.

> *A ball ... passed between my body and the right arm with which supported him [a patient], cutting through the sleeve and passing through his chest from shoulder to shoulder. There was no more to be done for him and I left him to his rest. I have never mended that hole in my sleeve. I wonder if a soldier ever does mend a bullet hole in his coat.*[1] —*Clara Barton*

How to Make a Sling

You will need:
  40" by 40" square of cloth

1. Hold your arm against your stomach so it makes the corner of a square.
2. Fold the square of cloth in half and slip one end of the cloth under the arm.
3. Bring the corner closest to you around the far side of your neck. Pull the other corner to behind your neck as well.
4. Tie the ends of the bandage behind your neck.

When you fold your bandage in half, experiment a bit. Does it work best as a rectangle (as shown to above) or as a triangle?

How to Make a Nurse's Apron

Supplies:

Piece of linen 14" wide by 18" long
Ribbon long enough to reach around your waist and tie a bow
Safety pin

1. Hem the bottom, top, and sides of the piece of linen.
2. Fold over ¼ inch of fabric on the top. Press, and then fold again to ¾ an inch. Press.
3. Sew along the bottom of the fold, leaving a space to thread the ribbon through.
4. Attach the safety pin to one end of the ribbon and thread the ribbon through the top of the apron.
5. Gather the apron to fit, and tie it around your waist with a bow.

Soon you'll have your own nurse's apron to wear while helping your wounded troops.

LINGO

Some terms were unique to Southern troops. Other terms were used by soldiers on either side of the line.

Argee—the pronunciation of the acronym RG, which stood for "rot gut," and was used to name any kind of inferior liquor.

Bone butter—a butter substitute used in many war prisons. Scraps of bone were boiled and then strained. As the broth cooled it hardened to a butter-like state.

Bought the farm—to have died on the field of battle.

Canaan, go to—to die; a biblical reference to the afterlife.

Chin music—slang for conversation.

Corked in a bottle, to be—a situation in which troops were trapped by opposition forces in a certain location.

Dandyfunk—a stew made of hardtack, molasses, and salt pork.

Dressed rats—rodents sold in Southern butcher shops when regular cuts of meat were unavailable.

Execute a flank movement—to attempt to frustrate body lice by turning one's underwear inside out.

Freight train—an incoming projectile, so called because of the screaming sound of the shell in flight.

Fresh Fish—new recruits.

Gallinipper—a large insect, usually a mosquito.

Hish and hash—a meal of whatever edibles were available.

Louse race—sometimes a louse race was their only form of entertainment available to soldiers. The race course was a saucer or plate, and three or more lice were placed in the center. The first louse to tumble off the edge was the winner.

McClellan pies—hardtack, nicknamed after Southern General George B. McClellan.

Niddering—cowardly.

Oysters—a southern dish made of cornmeal, eggs, and butter.

Pay a tribute to Neptune—a navy slang term for vomiting.

Pickled sardine—slang for a prisoner of war who had been imprisoned for several months.

Quaker gun—an imitation cannon made of wood, painted black, positioned to deceive the enemy.

Ramrod bread—cornmeal bread made by coating a cannon ramrod with a coating of cornmeal batter and baking over an open fire.

Sacred soil—Virginia mud.

Scuttlebutt—gossip. Referred to the butt or cask of fresh water around which sailors lingered and talked.

Sinks—latrines that were made by digging holes in the ground.

Those people—Robert E. Lee's usual reference to Union soldiers and Northern citizens.

Tough as a knot—in good health.

Wagon dog—a soldier who feigned illness to avoid combat.

Wolfhounds—ragged and worn Confederate soldiers.

Endnotes

Ch. 1

None

Ch. 2

1. From the diary of a Union soldier. Found in *Civil War,* by Martin W. Sandler, 38.
2. Worsham, *Foot Cavalry,* p. 98. Found in *Fighting Men of the Civil War,* by William C. Davis, 139.
3. Private Alpheris B. Parker, 10th Massachusetts Infantry, April 21, 1863.
4. www.baseball-almanac.com/articles/aubrecht.
5. Letter from a Union soldier, 1864, *Civil War,* 45.
6. *Life of BY,* 249–50.
7. Jas. O. Parker, Company H. 17th Regt. Miss. Vols." in *A While with the Blue: Memories of War Days,* by Benjamin Borton, 76–77, found in *Life of BY,* 355.
8. *Life of BY,* 174.
9. *Life of BY,* 153.

Ch. 3

1. *Life of BY,* p. 243.
2. From "A Fall Field Guide to Nuts," by Terry Krautwurst in *Mother Earth News,* Issue #113 Sept/Oct 1988.
3. *Commanders of the Civil War,* by William C. Davis, 65.
4. *Life of BY,* 246,

Ch.4

1. *Life of General Nathan Bedford Forrest,* by John A. Wyeth, 620.
2. *A Volunteer's Adventures, A Union Captain's Record of the Civil War,* by John William De Forest, edited by James H. Croushore, 63, found in *Life of BY,* 70.

Ch. 5

1. Frank Wilkie in *Fighting Men of the Civil War,* 50.
2. *JR,* 290.
3. *Fighting Men of the Civil War,* 58.
4. Wiley in *Life of BY,* 63.
5. *Fighting Men of the Civil War,* 59.

Ch. 6

None

Ch 7

1. From the correspondence of Clara Barton on www.nps.gov/anti/clara.htm/.

All: The majority of the historical photographs in this book may be found in the Library of Congress. To find these and other photographs, explore the American Memory: Selected Civil War Photographs collection on memory.loc.gov/ammem/cwphtml/cwphome.html.